JUST JOKING

STELLAR SPACE JOKES

by Joe Fullman

WINDMILL BOOKS

Published in 2017 by Windmill Books, an Imprint of Rosen Publishing
29 East 21st Street, New York, NY 10010

Text: Sally Lindley
Illustrations: Fabio Santomauro
Design: Trudi Webb
Editors: Joe Fullman and Joe Harris

CATALOGING-IN-PUBLICATION DATA
Names: Fullman, Joe.
Title: Stellar space jokes / Joe Fullman.
Description: New York : Windmill Books, 2017. | Series: Just joking | Includes index.
Identifiers: ISBN 9781508192640 (pbk.) | ISBN 9781508192589 (library bound) | ISBN 9781508192497 (6 pack)
Subjects: LCSH: Outer space--Juvenile humor.
Classification: LCC PN6231.J645 L563 2017 | DDC 818'.602--dc23

Manufactured in the United States of America
CPSIA Compliance Information: Batch #BS16PK: For Further Information contact Rosen Publishing, New York, New York at 1-800-237-9932

Contents

Alien Adventures! 4

Galactic Giggles! 16

UF-Ho Ho Ho! 32

Further Reading 48

Glossary 48

Index 48

Alien Adventures!

What do planets like to read?

Comet books.

Why should you never eat breakfast with an alien?

It might contain an Unidentified Frying Object!

Why are aliens green?

Because they're not ripe yet!

What do you call a pattern of stars in the sky that is anxious?

A consternation!

HOW CAN YOU TELL WHEN THE MOON HAS FINISHED ITS DINNER?

Because it's full!

Why couldn't the galaxy find its way home?

Because it didn't know the Milky Way!

If astronauts breathe oxygen during the day, what do they breathe at night?

Night-rogen!

What kind of music do astronauts like?

Rocket 'n' roll!

How can you tell if an alien has used your toothbrush?

It tastes like alien spit!

How do you get a robot to come to a party?

Send it a Tin-vitation.

How do robots sit at their desks?

Bolt upright!

What did the girl star say to the boy star?

I really glow for you!

What do you call an evil space tyrant walking in the sea?

Darth Wader!

Teacher: What is a light-year?

Student: The same as a normal year – but with fewer calories?

WHAT DO PLANETS SING AT KARAOKE PARTIES?

Nep-Tunes!

What do you call a piece of gum in space?

A Chew-FO!

What do you call a robot who knows a shortcut to somewhere?

R2-Detour!

What's the best way to see flying saucers?

Trip up a waiter!

Why can't you make a spacecraft out of sandpaper?

Because that would be science friction!

What do astronauts wear to weddings?

Spacesuits!

What does Jupiter use to hold up his jeans?

An asteroid belt!

What board game do astronauts like best?

Moon-opoly!

What do aliens use to shave?

A laser blade!

Where do the scariest aliens live?

In a far-off, distant terror-tory!

WHAT DO YOU CALL A SET OF TEETH ORBITING A STAR?

A molar system!

How do aliens cook humans?

They like them terri-fried!

Why did Mickey Mouse go to Neptune?

He was looking for Pluto!

What do alien poets write?

Uni-verses!

Where do alien aquatic mammals come from?

Otter space!

Did you hear that Albert Einstein developed a theory about space?

It was about time, too!

WHY WOULD AN ALIEN RATHER EAT A SHOOTING STAR THAN AN ASTEROID?

It's a little meteor!

Why didn't the alien eat the clown?

He said it tasted funny!

Planet: Are you joking?

Star: No, I'm Sirius!

Why should you never boil a space telescope?

Because it might Hubble over!

What did the alien cat say when it landed on Earth?

Take me to your litter!

Why are meals on spaceships so delicious?

Because the food is out of this world!

What do alien artists paint?

Mars-terpieces!

How do you find an alien with one eye?

It's not easy, you should try using both eyes!

What do you call an alien Santa sled?

A UF-Ho Ho Ho!

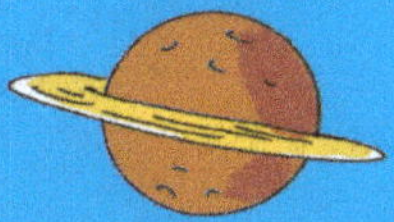

How do you get directions in space?

Askeroid!

What drink do aliens like best?

Gravi-tea!

Teacher: Why are you on the floor in front of Buzz Aldrin?

Student: I asked him if he was the first person on the Moon, and he said, "No, Neil before me."

What do you get if you cross a wizard with a spaceship?

A flying sorcerer!

What do you call an overweight alien?

An extra-cholesterol!

HOW DO YOU KNOW IF AN ALIEN IS JEALOUS?

It turns green!

Why did the astronaut cover his spaceship in mustard?

So the aliens couldn't ketchup with him!

Why did the astronaut build her spaceship out of feathers?

Because she wanted to travel light years!

What do you call a dishonest spacecraft?

A lying saucer!

How do you ride a space horse?

With a saddle-lite!

Knock, knock.

Who's there?

Jupiter.

Jupiter who?

Jupiter hurry, or you'll miss the school bus!

WHAT DO ALIENS HAVE FOR LUNCH?

Scream of tomato soup!

What steps should you take if you see an alien?

Large ones!

Teacher: What should you do if you find a spaceman?

Student: Park in it, man!

Why did the wannabe astronaut hit himself on the head?

So that he would see stars!

What was the sick alien's temperature?

Absolute zero!

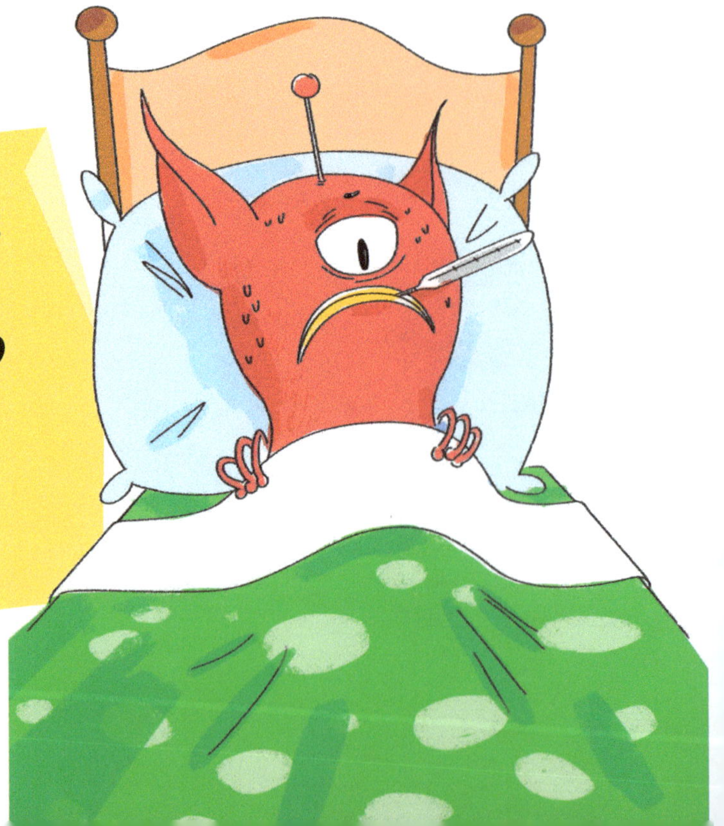

Why don't astronauts eat after they take off?

Because they've just had a big launch!

Why can't aliens remember anything?

Because everything goes in one ear and out the others!

How do aliens congratulate their teammates when they score a goal?

They give each other a high six!

What do you call alien speaking lessons?

Science diction!

Why is the universe so clean?

Because space is a vacuum!

Galactic Giggles!

HOW DO YOU KNOW SATURN IS MARRIED?

You can see its ring!

What do you call an insect on the Moon?

A lunar-tick!

Why is Mercury bald?

Because it has no 'air!

What keyboard key do astronauts use the most?

The space bar!

Why doesn't Luke Skywalker use a spoon?

Because he likes to use the forks!

What's the weakest part of space?

The puny-verse!

Why do astronauts wear bulletproof vests?

To protect themselves against shooting stars!

What do female aliens do when they want to get married?

They look for an edible bachelor!

Where do aliens go to study?

VERY high school!

Where do they go after that?

Universe-ity!

DO ROBOTS HAVE BROTHERS?

No, just transistors!

What do you call an insect in a spaceship?

An astron-ant!

I'd tell you a joke about space, but it's too out of this world!

Did you hear about the alien who wondered where the Sun went at night?

Eventually, it dawned on him!

What furry alien makes for a delicious snack?

A chocolate chip Wookiee.

Why are meteors very good at soccer?

Because they're shooting stars!

What did the alien race car driver say when it landed on Earth?

Take me to your speeder!

Which Egyptian pharaoh was also an astronaut?

Tutanka-moon!

What do you call a star's pet dog?

SuperRover!

What sweet treats do aliens like best?

Martian-mallows!

Where can you leave your spaceship when visiting a planet?

At a parking meteor!

Why do some aliens have twisted spaceships?

So they can travel at warp speed!

What sound does a space turkey make?

Hubble, Hubble, Hubble!

What advice should you always give to robots?

Look before you bleep!

WHAT DO YOU GET IF YOU CROSS AN ELF WITH A SPACESHIP?

A sate-sprite!

How do astronauts like their ice cream?

In floats!

Why shouldn't you be scared of a six-legged alien?

It's 'armless!

What do you call a shooting star that misses the Earth?

A meteor-wrong!

What do you call an almond in space?

An astro-nut!

What do you call a rodent that's gone to outer space?

A mouse-tronaut!

What do you get if you cross a robot with a comet?

An aster-droid!

How can you tell the Earth and the Moon are friends?

Because they've been going around together for years!

Where do astronauts keep their sandwiches?

In their launch-boxes!

What do you call a group of freezing planets?

A polar system!

HOW DO YOU KNOW IF THERE'S AN ALIEN IN YOUR HOUSE?

There'll be a spaceship parked in front!

Where do you keep alien fish?

In a planetarium!

What's the difference between a rocket and a fly?

A rocket can fly, but a fly can't rocket!

Why did the asteroid stop trying?

He didn't have enough comet-ment!

Where did the Apollo astronauts go to study?

A mooniversity!

How do astronauts see in the dark?

They turn on the satellite!

What Does the Moon Do When His Hair Gets Too Long?

Eclipse it!

What do you call a bowl of melted fudge flying through space?

A flying saucer!

What streaks across the night sky going "ka pow, ka pow"?

A shooting star!

What is the stupidest object in the night sky?

The Fool Moon!

What do astronomers use to keep their valuables safe?

Hubble wrap!

Why did the aliens land at the sports club?

So they could use their tennis rocket!

What did the planet say to the selfish star?

Not everything revolves around you!

Why was the alien bad at dancing?

It had three left feet!

Why did the spacecraft land a rover on Mars?

Just out of Curiosity!

How do you tip over a spaceship?

Rocket!

Why did the asteroid laugh at the shooting star?

It thought it was comet-y!

How can you tell if the Sun is happy?

It's beaming!

Why did the astronaut fly into the black hole?

He didn't understand the gravity of the situation!

How do aliens count to 50?

On their fingers!

HOW DO YOU ORGANIZE A SPACE PARTY?

You planet!

Which planet is hit by the most shooting stars?

Splaturn!

Why should you never trust atoms?

They make up everything!

What do you call a sick Martian?

An ailing alien!

What do you call a pattern of stars in the sky that feels sorry for you?

A consolation!

Why did the aliens call their baby Jupiter?

Because it was dense and gassy!

First alien: Do you like people?

Second alien: Yes... but I couldn't eat a whole one.

First alien: Yummy, more for me!

Why couldn't the black hole pass its exams?

Because it's super dense!

What do you call a spaceship covered in sugar and vinegar?

A sweet-and-sour saucer!

What did the alien plant say when it landed on Earth?

Take me to your weeder!

What did the lunar astronauts say when they bumped into each other?

I Apollo-gize!

What do you call an unhappy spaceship?

A crying saucer!

What do astronomers do to relax?

They take a Hubble bath!

What did the hungry alien say when it landed on Earth?

Take me to your feeder!

Teacher: How many balls of string would it take to reach the Moon?

Student: One, but it'd have to be a really big one!

What do aliens call junk food?

Unidentified Frying Objects!

Where do aliens do their gardening?

In greenhouses!

What do nuclear scientists have for dinner?

Fission chips!

What does an oversized alien wear?

A not-very-much-space suit!

Which star do you get if you crush an insect?

Betelgeuse!

What do you call a glass robot?

See-Through PO!

What did the alien robot say to the fuel pump?

Take your finger out of your ear when I'm talking to you!

Why are astronauts ambitious?

Because they want to go up in the world!

Why aren't astronauts practical?

Because they are not very down-to-earth people!

Which chocolate bar do astronauts like best?

Mars bars!

Why can't the Sun sing?

Because it's not a rock star!

UF-Ho Ho Ho!

WHY DID THE SUN GO TO SCHOOL?

To get brighter!

Why do astronauts worry about keeping their job?

Because they're always getting fired!

What do alien children do at Halloween?

They go from door to door dressed as humans!

What's green, has two heads, and goes up and down?

An alien stuck in an elevator!

What do you call an invisible evil space tyrant?

Darth Fader!

What do you call a spaceship made of herbs?

A thyme machine!

Where can you find black holes?

In black socks!

Where do astronauts go to learn how to fly in the darkness of space?

Night school!

What did the star who came last in the shining brightly competition get?

The constellation prize!

Did you hear about the astronaut who was reading a book on antigravity?

It was impossible to put down!

What do space monsters call humans?

Breakfast, lunch, and dinner!

Why did the astronomer change his mind about the Sun after looking at it through an ultraviolet telescope?

He saw it in a whole different light!

WHAT'S IN THE MIDDLE OF JUPITER?

The letter "i"!

What do you call a noisy spaceship?

A space racket!

What do you call a genuine spacecraft?

A True-FO!

What do aliens use to decorate their cakes?

Mars-ipan!

How can you tell Mars has a lot of books?

Because it looks well red!

What do you call a lazy astronaut?

A waste of space!

Did you hear about the satellite dishes that got married?

They had an amazing reception!

Where do aliens wash?

In a meteor shower!

WHY ARE ALIENS GOOD AT GARDENING?

Because they have green thumbs!

What do you call a recently built spaceship?

A New-FO!

What do you call an alien with two heads?

A two-headed alien!

When do astronauts like to eat?

At launch time!

What films do alien insects like?

Sci-Fly movies!

Which side of a spaceship passes closest to the Moon?

The outside!

Teacher: What's closer, the Moon or China?

Student: The Moon, because I can see the Moon at night from here, but I can't see China.

What do you call a spaceship that looks different all the time?

A dyeing saucer!

What do you do with a tired baby astronaut?

You rocket!

Which Dance Does Neil Armstrong Like Best?

The Moon Walk!

What do you say to an alien with two heads?

Hello to you, and hello to you, too!

Why are alien kitchens always very messy?

Because of all the flying sauces!

How many ears does Captain Kirk have?

Three: a right ear, a left ear, and a final frontier!

What do you call a space telescope that doesn't work?

Hubble trouble!

What do you call an alien with three eyes?

An Aliiien!

Why aren't parties on the Moon any fun?

There isn't much atmosphere!

What's the best way to talk to aliens?

From a long way away!

Why couldn't the alien book a room on the Moon?

Because it was full!

What did the planet say to the star?

You're looking stellar!

What do you call two spaceships flying together at exactly the same speed?

Tying saucers!

What did Jupiter say to Saturn?

Give me a ring sometime!

Why did Darth Vader cross the road?

To get to the Dark Side!

What's the most important quality needed to become an astronaut?

A good altitude!

Why are aliens good for the environment?

Because they're so green!

WHY DOESN'T THE SUN NEED TO GO TO COLLEGE?

Because it has a million degrees!

Why did the astronaut couple rent a new house?

They needed more space!

What's green and purple, has three heads and six arms, and goes "beep beep"?

An alien in a traffic jam!

What do shooting stars say when they greet each other?

Please to meteor!

What do you call a Jedi knight in a bubble bath?

Soapy-Wan Kenobi!

What did the alien tree say when it landed on Earth?

Take me to your cedar!

WHY DIDN'T THE DOG STAR LAUGH AT THE JOKE?

It was too Sirius!

Why did the astronaut throw eggs at the alien?

He wanted to eggs-terminate it!

What do you call the lights on a lunar spacecraft?

Moonbeams!

What do astronauts put in their sandwiches?

Launch-meat!

What do astronomers like to chew?

Hubble gum!

How should you serve tea to an alien?

On a flying saucer!

What should you do if you see an angry alien?

Give it some space!

Which dessert do rocket scientists like?

Apple pi!

What kind of fish live in space?

Nep-tuna!

What other kind of fish lives in space?

Starfish!

How do aliens play badminton?

With a space shuttlecock!

What do you call a spaceship that doesn't mind its own business?

A prying saucer!

Knock knock.

Who's there?

Saturn.

Saturn who?

Saturn front of this spaceship, waiting for it to take off!

Where do alien fish come from?

Trouter space!

WHAT DO ALIENS CALL ASTRONAUTS IN SPACESHIPS?

Canned food!

What do you call a sad spaceship?

An Unidentified Crying Object!

Why did the alien eat a flourescent lamp?

It wanted a light meal!

Why did the cow travel in the spaceship?

It wanted to go to the Moooon!

If there are Venus flytraps on Earth, does that mean there are Earth flytraps on Venus?

Why did the asteroid look both ways when crossing the road?

It had comet sense!

WHAT DO YOU CALL AN ALIEN WEARING PLATFORM HEELS?

A Shoe-FO!

What do you call an alien with no eyes?

Alen!

What do people on the Moon do after they get married?

They go on their Honey-Earth!

Why did the student say she wanted to be an astronaut?

She had high hopes!

What clothes do astronauts like best?

Apollo shirts!

What goes in one year and out the other?

A time machine!

What do you call an unsuccessful extraterrestrial?

A fail-ien!

What was the first animal in space?

The cow that jumped over the Moon!

But why did the cow jump over the Moon?

Because the farmer had cold hands!

What do you call a really scary alien?

An extra-terror-estrial!

Further Reading

Star Wars Joke Book. Egmont, 2015.

Weitzman, Ilana. *Jokelopedia*. Workman, 2013.

Woolley, Steph. *The Bumper Book of Very Silly Jokes*. Macmillan, 2013.

Glossary

Apollo The U.S.-run space missions that landed astronauts on the Moon between 1969 and 1972.

asteroid A small lump of rock that orbits the Sun.

astronaut Someone who travels into space from Earth.

astronomer A scientist who studies space.

comet A lump of rock and ice that travels through space with a long bright tail stretching out behind it.

constellation A group of stars that forms a pattern in the night sky.

Hubble A giant space telescope that orbits the Earth, taking pictures of space.

meteor A rock that enters Earth's atmosphere, burning up as a shooting star.

UFO An "Unidentified Flying Object"– something strange seen in the sky that some people believe might be an alien spacecraft.

Index

aliens 4, 5, 6, 8, 9, 10, 11, 12, 13, 14, 15, 17, 18, 19, 20, 21, 22, 23, 25, 26, 27, 28, 29, 30, 31, 32, 35, 36, 37, 38, 39, 40, 41, 32, 43, 44, 46, 47
Armstrong, Neil 12, 37
asteroids 8, 10, 11, 22, 26, 45
astronauts 5, 7, 8, 13, 15, 16, 17, 18, 19, 21, 22, 23, 24, 26, 28, 29, 31, 32, 33, 34, 35, 36, 40, 41, 42, 44, 46
astronomers 29, 34, 42
comets 4, 22, 26, 45
constellation 4, 33
Earth 19, 21, 22, 28, 29, 31, 37, 41, 46
flying saucers 7, 12, 13, 24, 28, 29, 37, 38, 39, 43, 44
Hubble 10, 20, 24, 29, 38, 42
Jupiter 8, 13, 27, 34
light-years 6, 13
Mars 11, 25, 27, 31, 35
meteors 10, 19, 20, 21, 35, 41
Moon 4, 12, 14, 16, 19,22, 23, 24, 29, 37, 39, 42, 45, 46, 47
Neptune 6, 9, 43
planets 4, 6, 8, 10, 11, 13, 16, 20, 22, 23, 25, 27, 31, 34, 35, 40, 44
robots 5, 6, 7, 18, 20, 22, 30, 31
rockets 5, 23, 25, 43
satellites 13, 20, 23, 35
Saturn 16, 27, 40, 44
shooting stars 10, 17, 19, 21, 24, 27, 33, 41
spacecraft / ship 7, 11, 12, 13, 18, 20, 22, 24, 28, 29, 34, 36, 37, 39, 42, 44, 45
stars 4, 6, 10, 17, 19, 21, 24, 25, 27, 30, 31, 33, 39, 41, 42
Sun 18, 26, 31, 32, 34, 40
telescopes 10, 34, 38
UFOs 4, 7, 24, 34, 36, 45, 46
universe 9, 15, 17